TOP SECRET SCIENCE IN

ENERGY

W9-BON-382

Megan Kopp

CRABTREE
PUBLISHING COMPANY
WWW.CRABTREEBOOKS.COM

TOP SECRET SCIENCE

Author: Megan Kopp

Editors: Sarah Eason, Honor Head, Harriet McGregor, and Janine Deschenes

Proofreaders: Sally Scrivener, Tracey Kelly, and Wendy Scavuzzo

Editorial director: Kathy Middleton

Design: Jeni Child

Cover design: Paul Myerscough and Jeni Child

Photo research: Rachel Blount

Production coordinator and prepress technician: Ken Wright

Print coordinator: Katherine Berti

Consultant: David Hawksett

Produced for Crabtree Publishing by Calcium Creative

Library and Archives Canada Cataloguing in Publication

Kopp, Megan, author
        Top secret science in energy / Megan Kopp.

(Top secret science)
Includes index.
Issued in print and electronic formats.
ISBN 978-0-7787-5993-5 (hardcover).--
ISBN 978-0-7787-5999-7 (softcover).--
ISBN 978-1-4271-2242-1 (HTML)

        1. Power resources--Research--Juvenile literature. I. Title.

TJ163.23.K67 2019   j333.79   C2018-905658-4
                                        C2018-905659-2

Library of Congress Cataloging-in-Publication Data

Names: Kopp, Megan, author.
Title: Top secret science in energy / Megan Kopp.
Description: New York, New York : Crabtree Publishing, [2019] |
    Series: Top secret science | Includes index.
Identifiers: LCCN 2018053384 (print) | LCCN 2018054836 (ebook) |
    ISBN 9781427122421 (Electronic) |
    ISBN 9780778759935 (hardcover : alk. paper) |
    ISBN 9780778759997 (pbk. : alk. paper)
Subjects: LCSH: Energy industries--Juvenile literature. |
    Energy policy--United States--Juvenile literature. |
    Power resources--Research--Juvenile literature.
Classification: LCC TJ163.23 (ebook) | LCC TJ163.23 .K67 2019 (print) |
    DDC 333.79--dc23
LC record available at https://lccn.loc.gov/2018053384

Crabtree Publishing Company
www.crabtreebooks.com   1-800-387-7650

Published in Canada
Crabtree Publishing
616 Welland Ave.
St. Catharines, ON
L2M 5V6

Published in the United States
Crabtree Publishing
PMB 59051
350 Fifth Avenue, 59th Floor
New York, NY 10118

Published in the United Kingdom
Crabtree Publishing
Maritime House
Basin Road North, Hove
BN41 1WR

Published in Australia
Crabtree Publishing
Unit 3 – 5 Currumbin Court
Capalaba
QLD 4157

CONTENTS

Chapter 1: **Who Controls Our Energy?** 4

Chapter 2: **The Fight for Energy** 10

Chapter 3: **Investing in the Future** 14

Chapter 4: **Nuclear Energy** 24

Chapter 5: **Cutting-Edge Energy** 32

Chapter 6: **What Next?** 40

Be an Energy Research Scientist 44

Glossary 46

Learning More 47

Index and About the Author 48

WHO CONTROLS OUR ENERGY?

Energy rules our daily lives. We use it when we get out of bed in the morning, when we travel to school, and when we play a video game. Energy is defined as the capacity or ability to do work.

ENERGY TYPES

Energy takes many forms. Electrical energy lights our homes and powers our devices. Heat energy cooks our food. Kinetic energy is present in moving objects. We need a source to make energy. Coal, gas, the Sun, and wind are all energy sources. Both **renewable** and **nonrenewable** energy sources are used to make electrical energy. Nonrenewable energy sources are those that will one day run out. **Fossil fuels**—oil, coal, and natural gas—are nonrenewable energy sources. They are burned in power plants to make electrical energy. Burning fossil fuels **pollutes** the environment and releases **greenhouse gases**, which warm Earth's temperature. Renewable energy sources are those that will not run out. They include the wind, the Sun, and moving water. These energy sources do not release harmful gases. Globally, demand for renewable energy grew more than 6 percent in 2017, but fossil fuel energy accounts for more than 80 percent of the total energy used.

Fossil fuels are burned to create energy in power plants such as this one. Harmful gases are released through the thin chimneys.

BURNING UP

The burning of fossil fuels releases carbon dioxide and other greenhouse gases. The gases build up in the **atmosphere**, trapping heat and causing **global warming**, which is a rise in Earth's temperature. In 2017, carbon **emissions** reached their highest-ever amount, at 32.5 gigatons. So why do renewable energy sources not take up more of our energy needs?

DARK SCIENCE SECRETS

Government representatives help decide what energy should be used, and how. But outside forces often try to sway their decisions in favor of a certain side. These outside forces are lobbyists—people who are paid by companies or organizations to try to **lobby**, or influence, government decisions. Both the oil and gas industry and environmental groups use lobbyists. Environmental groups lobby government representatives to reduce carbon emissions and increase the use of renewable energy sources. Oil and gas lobbyists try to gather support for such things as approval to build more pipelines. However, studies show that the oil, gas, and transportation organizations that rely on fossil fuels outspend environmental groups and the renewable energy sector by ten to one in lobbying budgets.

Organized protests about global warming also hope to change political opinion and actions.

ONE PLANET
ONE PEOPLE
ONE FUTURE

CRUDE OIL AND BIG BUSINESS

Crude oil is a thick liquid found beneath Earth's surface. We use oil products for everything from asphalt on roads to gasoline in vehicles to plastic in bread bags. Saudi Arabia and Russia each provide 13 percent of the world's supply of crude oil. The United States supplies another 12 percent, and Canada follows in fourth place at 5 percent. Governments and private companies play different roles in getting oil from the ground to the **consumers**, or the people who buy and use the oil.

OIL COMPANIES

In the United States and Canada, many oil production companies are independent and operate only in their home country. Some operate across North America. A few U.S. oil companies operate internationally, including ExxonMobil, Chevron, and ConocoPhillips. Oil production is big business. In 2018, ExxonMobil was estimated to be worth $344 billion. Chevron is worth $239 billion, and ConocoPhillips comes in at around $79 billion.

Oil pipelines transport oil to consumers. They often run through previously undisturbed landscapes.

There are almost half a million oil wells in the United States. Crude oil production rose 10 percent in 2017.

BIG WORLD OF OIL

Oil production companies are motivated by **profit**, or making a lot of money. To make as much money as possible, the companies want to develop oil resources quickly. In 2018, in the United States, oil production rose to its highest level in nearly 50 years. More than 10 million barrels a day were produced. Politics are driving this surge in U.S. oil production. The Trump administration proposed spending an extra $281 million on fossil fuel research and development in 2019. At the same time, it proposed cuts to programs designed to study and reduce the effects of **climate change**. It also wants to cut further research into forms of renewable energy.

DARK SCIENCE SECRETS

The U.S. Environmental Protection Agency (EPA) plays an important role in developing **policies** that can help the environment. In 2016, the EPA wrote a series of rules requiring oil and gas companies to limit **methane gas** emissions. In 2018, the changes made by the Trump administration meant that the EPA rules were weakened. This has made it easier for energy companies to release methane into the air. Methane gas is a powerful greenhouse gas and it greatly contributes to climate change.

REACHING OIL

Companies drill for oil on land and in **offshore waters**. Offshore drilling operations are conducted from oil rigs. These are platforms on which the drilling equipment is located. In 2018, the U.S. government said that they wanted to open up nearly all American offshore waters for potential oil and gas drilling.

Maggie carries a video camera and floodlights to check for cracks in underwater pipelines.

ROBOT POWER

Technological and scientific developments are expanding the search for new sources of oil. Scientific advances are also helping maintain current offshore oil rigs. BP has a large oil platform, called Thunder Horse, in the U.S. Gulf of Mexico. A dog-sized robot, the MaggHD (also known as Maggie), is used to check the underwater pipes at Thunder Horse. Maggie uses magnetic tracks to creep along the pipes that connect the surface platform to the seafloor. The robot inspects the pipes as it travels, using **ultrasound** and cameras. Other smart devices such as mini-submarines and **drones** are being used to replace workers in dangerous situations on oil rigs. For example, drones can be used to inspect exhaust systems instead of having a person climb high on an oil platform. They save lives and money.

HIDDEN DANGERS

In 2010, Deepwater Horizon became the most expensive offshore drilling disaster in U.S. history. The oil rig exploded and oil shot out uncontrollably. The well was plugged 87 days after the explosion, but 3.19 million barrels of oil had already polluted the Gulf of Mexico. It was the largest marine oil spill in history. By 2018, the cost of the cleanup, settling **lawsuits**, and other losses totalled a staggering $65 billion. Eleven people were killed and more than 1,300 miles (2,100 km) of shoreline, and coastal and ocean floor **habitats** were affected.

DARK SCIENCE SECRETS

Life on an oil rig has always been dangerous, but, today, new risks are emerging. **Cybercrime** costs offshore oil and gas companies millions of dollars every year in damaged equipment and lost production. In 2012, an employee at Saudi Arabian Oil Company opened an e-mail containing a virus. Computer files immediately disappeared and computers shut down. In a matter of hours, more than 30,000 computers were affected. The company was forced to temporarily stop selling oil because it could not process payments. Cyberattacks like this are a growing issue in oil and gas companies. The attacks can come from **activists** fighting for political and environmental causes, as well as **terrorists** trying to disrupt oil supplies.

After the Deepwater Horizon explosion, the U.S. government created important safety rules, but the current Trump administration wants to reverse them to save costs for oil companies.

CHAPTER 2

THE FIGHT FOR ENERGY

Fracking is a method of getting oil out of the ground. Tunnels are drilled into the ground, then water is pumped into them. This creates cracks in rock that contains oil and gas. The oil and gas in the rock is pushed closer to the surface, where they can be collected.

By tunneling in this way, oil and gas companies can frack much larger areas of rock to reach the valuable oil and gas they contain. The problem is that fracking causes earthquakes, disrupts the natural movement of water through rocks underground, and pollutes water sources with harmful chemicals.

COURT CASE

In 2016, the Sierra Club environmental group filed a federal lawsuit against three energy companies: Chesapeake Energy, Devon Energy, and New Dominion. The group said that these companies had placed people and the environment in Oklahoma and Kansas at risk from major human-made earthquakes caused by the companies' fracking waste disposal practices. During the case, the judge said that, "Every night, more than a million Oklahomans go to bed with reason to wonder whether they

Fracking allows companies to collect oil and gas previously locked in rock.

water

tunnel   layers of rock

rock containing oil or gas

fractures

Once fracking fractures have been made, pumping stops. The oil flows into the fractures and is removed through a well head, or the part of the well that is above ground.

will be awakened by muffled booms which precedes ... the shaking of the ground under their homes." However, the judge also stated that he felt decisions about the issue were not his to make. He said that the Oklahoma Corporation Commission (OCC) was responsible for regulating fracking and was already working on new rules to address earthquakes. The judge believed the organization should decide the outcome of the issue.

CANADIAN QUAKES

Fracking is responsible for almost 90 percent of earthquakes of more than magnitude 3.0 in western Canada, where the activity takes place. Albertan Jessica Ernst believes that fracking on her land released dangerous amounts of methane and other chemicals into her well. She first went to court in 2007 to have her case heard. As of 2017, after numerous attempts to find justice, she has not yet been successful.

DARK SCIENCE SECRETS

In Pennsylvania, from January 1, 2008, to September 20, 2016, fracking companies broke more than 4,351 rules and regulations meant to protect the environment and human health. Between 2007 and 2016, there were at least 283 cases of **contaminated**, or polluted, drinking water, as a result of drilling operations at fracking wells.

NOT IN MY BACKYARD!

The United States has the largest network of energy pipelines in the world. There are more than 2.4 million miles (3.9 million km) of pipelines, and around 72,000 miles (116,000 km) of them transport crude oil. Most of these are underground. One argument against using pipelines is that transporting oil can result in damaging leaks and spills. Over time, the metal used for pipelines **corrodes**, or is destroyed by chemical reactions. The metal **welding**, or joining, that holds sections of the pipeline together can fail, too. These are two ways pipelines can leak and spill.

PIPELINE SPILLS

The Pipeline and Hazardous Materials Safety Administration (PHMSA) collects data for U.S. pipeline spills. Since 2010, the organization estimates that close to 9 million gallons (34 million l) of oil has been spilled. In Canada, there were 41 percent more pipeline incidents in 2017 compared to 2016. The Keystone pipeline transports more than half a million barrels of crude oil products every day from Canada down to the Gulf Coast. Keystone was built in 2010 with new leak detection technologies, but that did not keep it from leaking. Most of the 14 leaks that occurred in its first year of operation were minor. One major leak occurred in North Dakota when 21,000 gallons (79,500 l) of oil were released. On November 16, 2017, a break in the pipeline saw about 5,000 barrels of crude oil spilled near Amherst, South Dakota.

In 2010, 1 million gallons (3.8 million l) of oil spilled from the Enbridge pipeline into Michigan's Talmadge Creek and the Kalamazoo River.

In 2017, President Trump signed orders giving the go-ahead for the Keystone XL pipeline.

KICKING UP CONTROVERSY

The Keystone pipeline is not to be confused with the new Keystone XL pipeline, although they are related. Keystone XL is a pipeline that would run 1,179 miles (1,900 km) from Canada to connect with the current Keystone pipeline. Construction of Keystone XL is protested by environmental groups and Native American tribes because of the damage it could do to the surrounding land—especially in Nebraska, where it could affect an underground water system called the Ogallala **aquifer**.

DARK SCIENCE SECRETS

Line 5 is an oil pipeline that was built in 1953. The pipeline crosses under the Straits of Mackinac, between Lake Huron and Lake Michigan. Line 5 carries about 23 million gallons (87 million l) of crude oil every day. Although Line 5 has not yet had a known leak in the Straits of Mackinac, there have been 29 spills on the land-based part of the pipeline. The waterway is heavily used by ships and boats. Environmental groups say the chances are high of a disastrous, underwater leak as a result of boat damage to Line 5. They also claim that the pipeline is old and a leak could result through wear and tear.

CHAPTER 3

INVESTING IN THE FUTURE

What is the answer to our energy demands? Many people think that the answer is renewable energy, in which energy from wind, sunshine, moving water, and the ground is harvested to make electricity.

CATCHING THE WIND

Wind farms feature huge wind turbines (right) which capture wind energy. But wind is more reliable at higher **altitudes**, which are measures of height from Earth's surface. Researchers are considering new ways of catching the wind, at altitudes much higher than a turbine can reach. National Aeronautics and Space Administration (NASA) researchers have spent $100,000 exploring the pros and cons of high-flying wind farms that are fixed to the ground.

Kite-like turbines could fly in the sky, sending power down to the ground through special cables. An Italian company called TWIND is developing a wind turbine farm using kite-like turbines. The turbines are balloons that have sails. The turbines are **tethered**, or tied, to the ground. The turbines will be positioned so that they float 30,000 feet (9,144 m) above ground, where they will capture wind energy.

By mid-2018, a record amount of wind farms were under construction across the United States.

WHAT ABOUT THE BIRDS?

Bird and bats **migrate**, or travel regularly from one place to another. Wind farms on their migration routes can be deadly. In Canada, it is estimated that more than 47,000 bats are killed by wind turbines each year. Wind turbines kill 140,000–328,000 birds in the United States each year. Imagine how many birds might be killed if wind power steps up to 20 percent of total U.S. energy—approximately 1.4 million birds might be affected. However, to put this into context, many more birds (between 365 and 988 million) are killed every year by flying into buildings, particularly into windows.

TOMORROW'S SECRETS

Offshore wind electricity in the European Union (EU) is projected to increase by 40 times its current level by 2030. The first-ever study looking at the impact of offshore wind power on **marine**, or ocean, systems was carried out in 2017. The results showed that blue mussels, which are normally found around coastlines (where they attach to land) are now also found out at sea, where they attach to offshore wind turbines. Mussels help other marine species because they absorb harmful chemicals, which makes the water cleaner. Creatures can also live on their shells. This may mean that more species will begin to live around offshore wind turbine farms.

ENERGY FROM THE SUN

Radiant energy is energy that travels as waves. The Sun's energy travels to Earth as waves. This renewable energy source becomes solar energy when we **harvest**, or catch, it using solar panels. There are two main types of solar technology: **photovoltaics (PV)** and **concentrated solar power (CSP)**. PV captures sunlight to make electricity. CSP harnesses the Sun's light and uses it to create **thermal energy** that powers heaters or turbines.

This solar farm near Austin, Texas, makes enough electricity to power 5,000 homes.

PV POWER

Solar panels are made up of smaller units called PV cells. These collect radiant energy. Researchers have made PV cells more and more **efficient**, which means that they produce more electricity and less waste. Today, PV cells are made of an ultrathin **film**. This film is about 1/100th of the width of a human hair. The cells are so light that they could sit on top of a soap bubble without making it burst! They easily bend, so they can be used in curves and corners.

Tiny channels on the thin film help convert the sunlight to electricity. A research team is currently looking at using **lasers** to create the channels. They have found a technique that can create channels with precision and speed. It is hoped that this will make thin-film PV cells even more efficient and less costly to build.

IMPROVING PV CELLS

The solar panels built today are up to 23.5 percent efficient. This means they can convert almost one-quarter of the sunlight that hits them into electricity. In 2018, researchers at the Massachusetts Institute of Technology (MIT) announced a new technology that could double the overall efficiency of solar cells. This new technology captures and uses the waste heat that is normally given off by solar panels. This massively improves their energy efficiency.

These solar trees (see below) may one day be replaced with more realistic-looking, leafy power producers.

TOMORROW'S SECRETS

Researchers at the VTT Technical Research Centre of Finland have developed **three-dimensional (3-D)** printed solar energy trees. Each leaf is a flexible solar cell. The leaves **generate**, or make, and store solar energy. The more leaves, the more energy the tree can harvest. The trees work both indoors and outdoors. They can also harvest energy from the wind and from temperature changes in the environment.

ENERGY FROM EARTH

Below Earth's **crust**, or rocky outer layer, there is heat. It is produced when **minerals** break down deep underground. Heat also rises from Earth's hot center. This heat energy is called **geothermal energy**. It can be harvested and used to provide heat and make electricity.

USING GEOTHERMAL ENERGY

To **extract**, or take out, geothermal energy, deep wells are drilled into Earth's crust. Water heated by geothermal energy fills the wells and is used to heat buildings. Geothermal energy can also be used to produce electricity in a geothermal plant. This technology is used in areas that have a lot of active volcanoes or in areas where two parts of Earth's crust are shifting next to one another. This is why most geothermal power plants are found in parts of the world, such as Iceland, Indonesia, and Ecuador, that experience many earthquakes or have a lot of volcanoes.

Geothermal energy provides around 13 percent of New Zealand's electricity.

IS IT RENEWABLE?

If managed properly, geothermal energy is a renewable resource because it produces electricity from the natural heat of Earth. Geothermal power has little or no greenhouse gas emissions. But there are still risks. Developing geothermal resources can bring up hazardous gases. Other dangerous materials, such as arsenic and mercury, can also come up to Earth's surface with the hot water.

In July 2018, the U.S. government announced it would provide $3.6 million for research and development of **machine learning** in geothermal energy. Machine learning is a branch of **artificial intelligence (AI)** in which computer systems learn from data, identify patterns, and make decisions with very little human input. It is efficient and time saving. Machine learning is being used to find new geothermal sources by analyzing minerals in the ground.

DARK SCIENCE SECRETS

In Pohang, on November 15, 2017, the most damaging earthquake in South Korea's history occurred. Geothermal energy production may have been to blame. Fracking can be used in geothermal energy production to push hot water below ground closer to the surface, where it can be easily accessed. However, the water injected deep underground during fracking can trigger earthquakes. This is because the water seeps into cracks below Earth's surface and causes them to move. In the case of the Pohang earthquake, fracking water was injected right on top of a **fault line**, an area where two sections of Earth's crust meet. This may have caused the earthquake to take place.

The Pohang earthquake injured 90 people and caused $52 million in damage.

GAS TRAPPING

Carbon capture and storage (CCS) is a new technology developed to reduce the quantity of greenhouse gas emissions entering the atmosphere. In this technology, huge fans capture emissions from the burning of fossil fuels. The gases are passed through a watery solution that pulls out and traps carbon dioxide. It can capture up to 90 percent of the carbon dioxide emissions from burning fossil fuels.

Today in Lake Nyos (see below), scientists reduce the risk of huge carbon dioxide leaks by piping gas-rich water from the lake bed to the surface. There, the carbon dioxide is released in harmless amounts.

HOW IT WORKS

The technology has three parts. First, the carbon dioxide is captured. Second, it is transported by ship or pipeline to a storage site. And finally, it is securely stored underground in old oil and gas fields, or deep in underground rock that also holds salty water. People against the technology are concerned about what would happen if there was a sudden release of this stored carbon dioxide. A similar release happened naturally when massive amounts of carbon dioxide erupted from Lake Nyos in Cameroon in 1986. Seventeen hundred people died, along with thousands of cattle and many birds and other animals.

WHEN WILL IT HAPPEN?

Scientists are working on CCS technology to see if it can be effective and affordable. It may be one way of reducing greenhouse gases and preventing Earth from overheating. It is a huge challenge. Large-scale CCS does not yet exist. The U.S. government signed a budget bill in 2018 that encourages organizations to capture and store emissions.

The technology necessary for capturing carbon is expensive. Because of this new bill, companies who take the first steps toward capturing carbon will save a lot of money on their **taxes**, or money they pay to the government. As more and more companies do this, the technology will improve and the cost of CCS will come down.

TOMORROW'S SECRETS

Carbon Engineering is an energy company backed by Microsoft founder Bill Gates. The company has proven that it can turn a carbon-dioxide-rich watery solution into an alternative fuel. It heats and treats the solution, and takes out chemicals needed for fuel—including gas, diesel, and jet fuel. The next step will be to turn this technology into an affordable product that can be sold.

Burning jet fuel in the airline industry accounts for 3 to 9 percent of the total climate change caused by humans.

NANOTECHNOLOGY

Nanotechnology is the science of super-small things. A nanometer is 3.2 billionths of a foot (1 billionth of a meter). Most nanotechnology materials range in scale from 1 to 100 nanometers (nm). This is such a small scale that it is almost impossible to imagine. Over the last decade, a wide variety of nanomaterials have been manufactured and used in products ranging from cosmetics to electronics to building materials. Researchers are now looking into tiny, yet smart, nanotechnology energy options.

SMART TECH

Smart **textiles**, or fabrics, are turning body movements into power sources. Scientists around the world have already shown how a piece of smart fabric can be used to charge a phone with simple body movements and surrounding light.

It uses **nanofibers**, or teeny, tiny fibers. These lightweight fibers are coated with a thin layer of **conducting** material, which allows the fabric to create energy through friction. The material could also be used to create larger energy-generating structures, such as curtains or tents.

Currently, a group of U.S. researchers is working on using tiny nanosheets of **black phosphorus**. Bending or pressing the sheets creates a small **electrical current** that can be collected and stored in a battery. The sheets are so thin that they can be added to fabric without changing the look or feel of the material.

These fitness socks have built-in fibers that monitor the speed and motion of the wearer.

ENERGY FROM AIR

Hydrogen is an **element**. When combined with oxygen, water is created. Water is present in the air we breathe. Researchers in Belgium have created a device to pull hydrogen from air. The device has two compartments separated by a nano-thin wall. Air is broken down in one compartment. Some of the materials from the breakdown, including hydrogen, pass into the wall. Nanomaterials in the wall pull out the hydrogen and collect it in the second chamber. The hydrogen can be harvested and stored as a potential fuel source.

Currently, little is known about the potential impact of nanoparticles on the environment and human health. Researchers are looking into the effects of human and environmental exposure to nanomaterials.

TOMORROW'S SECRETS

University of Wisconsin-Madison materials engineers have developed a type of flooring that can convert footsteps into electricity. The flooring is partly made up of nanofibers. When a person walks on the floor, it forces the nanofibers to rub against each other. The contact between the fibers produces electricity. Wires in the flooring then transmit the electricity to nearby lights and batteries, to power or charge them. The engineers who created the flooring are working on power-generating shoes.

CHAPTER 4

NUCLEAR ENERGY

release of energy   chain reaction
nucleus

splitting of nucleus

Nuclear energy, or atomic energy, is stored inside the nucleus, or central part, of an **atom**. Atoms are the **particles**, or tiny pieces, from which everything is made. Nuclear energy holds the atom's nucleus together. Nuclear power plants harvest nuclear energy by splitting apart the atoms of **uranium**, which is a metal found in rocks around the world. This process is called nuclear **fission**. The energy from nuclear fission is captured as heat and converted into electricity. Scientists are learning how to control another type of nuclear reaction called **fusion**. Fusion occurs when two atoms join together. Fusion also releases large amounts of energy.

In nuclear fission, a nucleus is split and a chain reaction begins. In a chain reaction, the first splitting causes at least one more nucleus to be split.

WHAT IS THE WORRY?

Radiation is energy moving through space in the form of waves and particles. Radiation is a natural energy found in, around, and above the world we live in. There are many types of radiation. One type is called **ultraviolet (UV)**, which the Sun gives out as visible light and can cause sunburn. Another type, known as X-ray, was not discovered until 1895. However, it can cause chemical changes in living things. High exposure is very dangerous. It can cause **radiation sickness**, cancer, and even death.

REACTOR ACCIDENTS

In 1986, an explosion at a nuclear reactor in Chernobyl, Ukraine, killed two workers, and 134 plant staff and emergency workers were affected by acute radiation sickness. Of these, 28 died within a few months. About 5 million people in the region were exposed to radiation, and more than 5,000 children developed cancer.

In 2011, there was a massive earthquake off the coast of Japan. It caused damage to the Fukushima nuclear power station. More than 100,000 people were evacuated from areas surrounding the reactors, and around 1,000 people died as a result of the disaster. Research is ongoing for long-term health effects from possible radiation exposure.

Uranium mining is a destructive process. The mines, such as this one in Australia, can badly damage the environment.

DARK SCIENCE SECRETS

Uranium **ore**, used in nuclear fission, is mined. One way to get the ore out of the ground involves pushing a special solution of water into the ground. The water is mixed with extra oxygen and carbon dioxide. The water solution breaks down the uranium, and mixes with it. The liquid mixture is then pumped back up to ground level, and the uranium in the liquid is removed. The remaining liquid mixture then goes back into the ground, to break down more uranium. The problem is that when the liquid mixes with clean water below the ground, it can contaminate it. Because it has mixed with uranium, the liquid can also become dangerously **radioactive**.

THE MANHATTAN PROJECT

During World War II (1939–1945), President Theodore Roosevelt set up the Manhattan Project. This was the code name for an effort to develop an **atomic weapon**. An atomic weapon is one that uses nuclear fission reaction to suddenly release massive amounts of energy. At the time, the Manhattan Project was a government secret. Few people knew about it.

WAR TO PEACE

On August 6, 1945, the first of two atomic bombs was used on Japan. Around 80,000 people were killed during the explosion. Tens of thousands later died from radiation sickness. But after the war, the U.S. government looked to nuclear energy for peaceful purposes. The Atomic Energy Commission (AEC) was set up in 1946. The nuclear fission technology perfected by the Manhattan Project became the basis for the creation of nuclear reactors for making electricity and for powering navy ships. In 1951, the Experimental Breeder Reactor in Idaho generated the first electricity from a nuclear reactor in the United States.

This image shows the first successfully exploded atomic bomb during a test explosion on July 16, 1945 in New Mexico.

THE LEGACY

Today, a Civilian Nuclear Program at Los Alamos, New Mexico, focuses on nuclear energy research and development. All data from the research is stored at the Los Alamos National Laboratory. Scientists there are trying to find out more about uranium.

Further research into nuclear energy is also being carried out at Oak Ridge, Tennessee. This was formerly a secret government town run by the AEC in the 1940s. Today, the Department of Energy's (DoE's) Oak Ridge National Laboratory is a leader in research into fusion energy.

In the 1940s, these large buildings held electrical equipment at the Manhattan Project's Oak Ridge site.

DARK SCIENCE SECRETS

It is not often talked about, but the Manhattan Project used Canadian uranium in the world's first atomic bombs. Canada **refined**, or made purer, and supplied uranium for use in top secret facilities in the United States during World War II. Eldorado Gold Mining Company reopened a closed mine located near Great Bear Lake in the Northwest Territories to supply the U.S. military with the uranium it needed to produce the atomic bomb. Canada continued to supply uranium for another 20 years after the war, for use in nuclear reactors in navy ships and for the production of electricity.

NEGATIVE ENERGY

Nuclear energy does not come without a cost. Equipment that has been used to create nuclear energy is radioactive for years after use. This makes it difficult to dispose of. So, how do you get rid of hazardous radioactive waste? In the past, the solution for disposing of this material was to load it into containers and dump it into the Pacific Ocean. The EPA has records showing that more than 55,000 containers were dumped at three separate sites off the east coast of the United States between 1946 and 1970.

RADIOACTIVE STORAGE SOLUTIONS

The United States alone currently has more than 100,000 tons (90,700 mt) of nuclear waste in need of disposal. That is enough to fill a football field about 65.6 feet (20 m) deep. For the most part, this waste is stored where it was generated—at 80 sites in 35 states. The waste must be continuously cooled because it continues to generate extreme heat and dangerous levels of radiation.

Radioactive waste is labeled with this unique symbol.

The waste is stored in special containers made of thick, super-strong concrete and lined with steel. The 40-foot (12 m) deep containers are filled with water. The radioactive material is carefully placed in this cooling bath. It takes at least three years for waste to cool down enough to be moved to dry container storage. There is still no permanent disposal site in the United States.

Transporting nuclear waste to secure storage sites requires special containers like this one.

TOMORROW'S SECRETS

There are people who believe that safe, environmentally friendly nuclear reactors are possible. Nuclear engineers in a Boston-based business called Transatomic Power are working toward that goal. If today's power plants lose power and backup power, the cooling systems stop working. Transatomic Power has created a reactor that automatically shuts down during a power outage. The fuel drains into an escape tank and is frozen solid. This stops a **meltdown**. To help solve the problem of what to do with used control rods, Transatomic's idea is to use them again in their next-generation molten, or liquid, salt nuclear reactor.

Molten salt reactors are fueled by uranium dissolved in liquid salt. It uses fuel more slowly and efficiently. It is also the perfect solution for using up the store of leftover, radioactive waste. The engineers at Transatomic Power hope to have a trial model built by the 2020s, and a commercial reactor up and running by the 2030s.

14:30 PM

WARNING, WARNING!

In June 2018, the DoE announced funding to support advanced nuclear reactor power plants. Up to $24 million was set aside for technologies to create lower cost, but safer, nuclear plant designs. Nuclear power already generates 15 percent of Canadian energy and nearly 20 percent of U.S. electricity. The United States is the world's largest producer of nuclear energy.

Some scientists are worried that the current storage of nuclear waste is a ticking time bomb. What would happen if there was an earthquake at a storage site? The Nuclear Regulatory Commission is betting on the fact that an earthquake big enough to trigger a radiation leak would never happen in a million years.

DISASTERS AND DRAGON KINGS

In 1979, a partial meltdown of a nuclear reactor at Three Mile Island, Pennsylvania, was the most serious nuclear accident in the United States. The small amount of radioactive material released had no detectable health effects on any of the plant workers or the public. It was classified as a "nuclear event." The term "dragon-king" refers to extreme nuclear

DARK SCIENCE SECRETS

The Chernobyl nuclear disaster is one of the most highly recognized examples of nuclear destruction. The area near the disaster still remains empty.

Yucca Mountain lies in a remote section of the Mojave Desert, about 80 miles (130 km) northwest of Las Vegas, Nevada. It was chosen as a permanent underground storage site for nuclear waste in 1987. It was supposed to open in 1998. But changing governments and strong opposition to the idea kept the project on hold. In 2011, the Obama administration officially turned the project off. In 2017, the Trump administration announced that they were going to restart the approval process for Yucca Mountain. Deep within the mountain, tunnels would house radioactive waste for a least the next 10,000 years. In June 2018, the house voted overwhelmingly in favor of moving ahead with the process. One month later, the efforts hit an obstacle. Funding was stopped by Congress. The battle is over, for now, but the process could restart in years to come.

events such as the Fukushima event in 2011. One scientific study from 2015 looked at the data from more than 200 nuclear energy accidents and incidents around the world. They found that there was a 50 percent chance of a dragon-king event in the next 60 to 150 years. There is a chance that a Three Mile Island event, or larger, could happen every 10 to 20 years.

Tunnels lead to the underground waste facility deep below Nevada's Yucca Mountain.

CHAPTER 5

CUTTING-EDGE ENERGY

PV cells have been used in solar energy plants for decades. Ninety percent of these contain **silicon**, but now there is a challenger in the research corner. New perovskite cells are more efficient and cheaper to make than the silicon cells. Silicon solar cells have around 20 percent efficiency. Perovskites are expected to have a 50 percent efficiency rating, which is significantly better.

The perovskite crystals in this glass cube glow green in the dark.

PEROVSKITE POWER

Perovskite solar cells are made from materials such as ammonia and iron. Perovskites soak up light over a wider range of **wavelengths**. This means they can turn more sunlight into electricity. They are lightweight, flexible, and **semitransparent**, or partially see-through. Researchers at Stanford University are going one step further and are experimenting with cells containing both perovskites and silicon. They stacked perovskites onto silicon and improved the system's ability to make electricity. This research may allow current users to upgrade their solar panels without the extra cost of full replacement. The technology is not yet on the market, but watch for it coming soon.

SOLAR TECH

Solar skin is a new product that uses lightweight and flexible cells. It makes it possible for solar panels to match the look of a roof, making them virtually invisible. In 2017, testing began on a new PV technology for use on solar-powered roads. This includes LED bulbs that can light up a road at night, and heat strips that melt snow during the winter.

THE FUTURE IS HOT!

In Iceland, scientists have begun drilling wells directly into volcanoes to investigate harnessing the power of **magma**, the hot molten rock beneath Earth's crust. In 2017, one well reached nearly 3 miles (4.8 km) deep. Temperatures there are hotter than in most geothermal wells, which means they could provide 10 times the potential power of other geothermal sources.

Power plants in Iceland often rely on energy provided by volcanic and geothermal sources.

DARK SCIENCE SECRETS

Most energy options, including renewable, feed into a main **energy grid** for use by consumers. In March 2018, the United States blamed Russia for cyberattacks on the U.S. energy grid. Hackers were actively trying to get into the country's energy, nuclear, water, and other industry sectors. Russia denies the claims. No one knows the exact reason for the hacking. It could have been spy-related, or perhaps it was an attempt to **sabotage** the country's energy sources.

FUEL CELL TECH

Hydrogen **fuel cells** create electricity using oxygen from the air and hydrogen from a tank. The fuel cells convert the hydrogen and oxygen into water, which makes it an environmentally friendly idea. The process was originally developed in the late 1800s, but it was not until a few years ago that fuel cells became a promising option to replace car batteries. A fuel cell is similar to a battery in terms of power, but batteries do not last forever. Fuel cells, on the other hand, keep making electricity as long as there is hydrogen in the tank.

BREAKTHROUGHS

Fuel cell technology exists but is still **evolving**, or changing, and there have been a few recent breakthroughs. Hydrogen-powered fuel cells use electrochemical reactions to make electricity. In electrochemical reactions, chemical energy is turned into electrical energy but without **combustion**, or burning. Materials called catalysts are needed to make the reactions work efficiently.

Hydrogen buses use fuel cell technology. In 2017, delivery companies FedEx and UPS switched to hydrogen power.

Toyota is planning
to use fuel cells
in its vehicles.

Platinum metal is the most common catalyst in vehicle fuel cells. It is expensive, costing around $66,000 per pound ($30,000 per kg). A team of engineers at the University of Delaware have developed a catalyst of a chemical **compound**, or blend, of tungsten carbide. It costs just $330 per pound ($150 per kg). This technology could make fuel cells cheaper and damage-resistant. Fuel cells are also expensive because they are produced in small amounts. Once they become more popular, the price will drop.

TOMORROW'S SECRETS

Some people have raised concerns about fuel cells. They feel that it does not make sense to use energy to produce hydrogen for a fuel cell when the energy could be used to simply charge a battery instead. Others, such as Amazon founder, Jeff Bezos, are embracing fuel cell technology. Amazon is looking into buying part of a company called Plug Power, which makes hydrogen fuel cells. Amazon is also buying fuel cells to power forklift vehicles in some of its warehouses. Many companies are watching Amazon's progress and the developments in fuel cell technology with interest.

LARGE HADRON COLLIDER

Energy comes in many forms and scientists are interested in them all. The Large Hadron Collider (LHC) is the world's largest and most powerful machine. The LHC is found close to 330 feet (100 m) underground beneath the border of France and Switzerland. It is a **particle accelerator**—a machine that speeds up particles close to the speed of light and smashes them together.

ACCELERATION

Particle accelerators were first used by physicists to look into the structure of an atom's nucleus. Since then, these machines have grown in size, leading up to the LHC. Particle accelerators use strong magnets to create high-speed energy **collisions**, or crashes. The bigger the accelerator, the faster the particles can travel, and the higher energy the collisions can be. LHC is a massive circular machine measuring 16.8 miles (27 km) around. It gets the energy it needs by flinging particles called protons in opposite directions at a little slower than the speed of light.

The LHC is a complicated series of tubes in an underground system.

FEAR OF THE UNKNOWN

The LHC made some people very uneasy. When the LHC was still in the development stage, a lawsuit was filed to stop it. It was filed by a retired radiation safety officer and a science writer. People were worried that smashing **subatomic particles**, or particles smaller than an atom, together at the speed of light could create **black holes**. This would collapse and destroy our world. Luckily, this did not happen! The lawsuit was dismissed.

TOMORROW'S SECRETS

So far, the LHC has discovered several new particles previously unknown to science. But by the end of 2018, it will have collected only about 3 percent of the data it is expected to deliver over the lifetime of the facility. The facility closed at the end of 2018 for major upgrades and renovations. At the end of 2020, LHC will restart as a much more powerful space research machine. It will use more intense beams and higher energy. Who knows what it will uncover about the energetic start and makeup of our universe.

The LHC contains about 9,600 magnets. Some weigh several tons each.

DARK ENERGY

The Fermi National Accelerator Lab (Fermilab) in Batavia, Illinois, is the U.S. headquarters for **particle physics**. It works with other sites around the world, including the LHC. Fermilab's particle accelerator is called the Tevatron. It was the second-most powerful accelerator in the world before it shut down in 2011. Research is not over, though. Fermilab scientists continue their research at the LHC. Fermilab scientists also now reach deep into space where **dark energy** exists.

WHAT IS DARK ENERGY?

Scientists at Fermilab and other institutions are mapping a portion of the southern sky. They are recording hundreds of millions of space objects in never-before-seen detail. The goal is to understand the mysterious force known as dark energy. Dark energy makes up the majority of our universe. Scientists believe that dark energy is the reason our universe is still **expanding**, or growing bigger, at a rapid rate when **gravity** should be slowing it down.

In 2017, a new telescope, the Canadian Hydrogen Intensity Mapping Experiment (CHIME), was installed near Penticton, BC. It is helping scientists understand more about the shape and structure of the universe.

VIEWING GALAXIES

The Dark Energy Survey (DES) is a project worked on by more than 400 scientists from seven different countries. Scientists involved want to create a detailed map of **galaxies** across our universe, and learn more about the dark energy that exists there. The Dark Energy Camera is key to the survey. It is now mounted on a telescope in Chile, South America. The camera can see light from galaxies billions of **light-years** away, allowing scientists to create the map. Another DES experiment looks at **muons**. A muon is a subatomic particle found in **cosmic rays**. Muons help scientists explore extremely high energies.

TOMORROW'S SECRETS

Nature produces particle accelerators called cosmic rays. Cosmic rays are bits of atoms that fall to Earth from outside our Solar System. They have far more energy than a particle in any man-made particle accelerator. Scientists are still investigating the source of ultra-high-energy cosmic rays. Unlocking the secrets of how cosmic rays work will happen someday.

CHAPTER 6

WHAT NEXT?

Fusion energy powers the Sun and all of the stars in the universe. Reproducing this on Earth, even on a small scale, would create a never-ending source of clean, cheap energy. Fusion happens when a gas is heated and separated into **ions** and **electrons**. Ions are atoms that carry an electrical charge. The overheated ions bump into one another and **fuse**, or join together, as one. This process releases energy that is three to four times as powerful as a fission reaction.

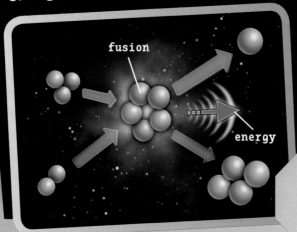

A nuclear fusion reaction creates both heat and light energy.

SKUNK WORKS

During World War II, in 1943, a secretive project began in the United States to build a jet fighter. Due to lack of space, the project operated out of a rented circus tent next to a manufacturing plant that had a strong smell. The project got the name "Skunk Works."

Today, the Skunk Works team is on the cutting-edge of all kinds of technology, including fusion. Their plan is to create a fusion reactor small enough to fit on a truck, but powerful enough to supply electricity to a community of up to 100,000 people.

FUSION NOW?

Skunk Works has been researching fusion for more than 60 years. Its small fusion reactor would mimic the process that the Sun uses to make energy. This would allow us to make fusion energy for use here on Earth. The heat energy created in the reactor would drive generators to create electricity.

In the United Kingdom, a mini fusion reactor has already successfully reached temperatures as hot as the Sun. The private company that created it, Tokamak Energy, hopes to start supplying fusion energy in 2030.

Stars, like our Sun, use fusion energy to create heat and light that travel across space.

TOMORROW'S SECRETS

A team of researchers at the University of New South Wales in Australia are shaking things up. They have created a new reactor design that uses different elements and methods to heat up its core 200 times hotter than the Sun. This energy positive fusion reactor does not exist yet, but its strange globe shape could be a game-changer. In theory, the round shape should mean that the reactor produces more energy than it uses. Scientists are watching with interest to see if it is successful.

FISSION/FUSION MIX

Fission, fusion—it is difficult to figure them out! Imagine what would happen if you mixed the two together. That is what China hopes to do with its **hybrid** fission/fusion reactor.

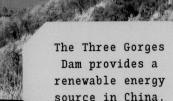

The Three Gorges Dam provides a renewable energy source in China.

CLEANER ENERGY

The idea to combine nuclear fusion and fission in one reactor has been around for at least 50 years. Research on the topic has been done in Russia, Europe, the United States, and Japan. China, though, is currently the only country thought to be looking into building a hybrid reactor. The project is supposed to be developed at the Chinese Academy of Engineering Physics in Sichuan. It is a top secret military research facility where China's nuclear weapons are built. The hybrid reactor project is part of the country's plan to replace fossil fuels with cleaner energy sources. In 2015, almost three-quarters of China's electricity was produced from fossil fuels, mostly coal. The massive Three Gorges and Yellow River hydroelectric projects account for 4 percent of the country's electricity.

With a population of more than 1.4 billion people, China is in need of power sources provided by facilities such as the Daya Bay nuclear plant.

In November 2014, China announced that by 2030, it would produce 20 percent of its electricity from non-fossil fuels. Nuclear reactors are gearing up to take over.

BIG BENEFITS

Traditional fission reactors produce radioactive waste products. Mainland China has more than 40 nuclear power reactors in operation, with around another 20 under construction and more about to start construction. Most of the waste produced in these fission reactors is stored inside the nuclear power plants. A hybrid fission/fusion reactor would use all but 1 percent of the fuel. It would also help reduce China's uranium shortage—the substance needed in nuclear reactors. The country has enough of the resource to meet its needs for about the next 100 years. A much more efficient hybrid reactor would mean that China would have enough uranium to last several thousand years. It is hoped that a test hybrid reactor could be running by 2030.

TOMORROW'S SECRETS

Traditional nuclear power plants produce a lot of waste. The proposed hybrid reactor will help deal with this problem because it will use nuclear fusion to burn waste products. So far, China has yet to produce a functional fusion reactor. That would be the natural first step before moving forward with plans for a fission/fusion hybrid.

BE AN ENERGY RESEARCH SCIENTIST

Renewable resources such as wind, water, and solar power are important for reducing greenhouse gas emissions. Technological advances will make them more affordable and more efficient in the future. Nonrenewable resources such as oil, gas, and coal will run out one day. Burning fossil fuels is also harmful to the environment. Nuclear energy is potentially hazardous, although scientists continue to work to find new ways around these dangers. It is clear that we need new energy sources. How would you go about developing one?

YOUR MISSION

- How will you go about finding an energy source? Research sources that are easy to find and extract or are in good supply. Perhaps there is a type of waste that could be used? What kind of energy production is most common near where you live?

- What research will you do? You might look around your home, your town, or research online or in the library.

- What factors do you need to consider? It is important that the new energy source does not damage the environment. Can you think of a source that might even benefit the natural world?

- What have you learned in this book about the **ethical** aspects of new energy sources? What are the potential effects of your source? Might it cause harm or problems for groups of people or the natural world?

Particle acceleration in the LHC is the future now. What will be the next new source of energy?

TOP SECRET

New ideas for energy production can be extremely valuable. Would you keep your research a secret? Would it be better to share the idea with others to make your idea even better? Explain your answers.

GLOSSARY

Please note: Some **bold-faced** words are defined where they appear in the book.

activists People who push to bring about political or social change

aquifer A place in the rock through which groundwater travels

artificial intelligence (AI) Computer systems that can perform tasks normally carried out only by humans

atmosphere The "blanket" of gases surrounding a planet

black holes Areas of space that have such strong gravity that nothing can escape them

black phosphorus An element that can conduct electricity

climate change A change in worldwide or local climate patterns due to an increase in levels of carbon dioxide in the atmosphere

conducting The transfer of energy in the form of heat or electricity

cosmic rays Highly energetic particles that travel through space

crude oil Unrefined oil

cybercrime Criminal activities carried out using computers or the Internet

dark energy An unseen force that counteracts gravity and causes the universe to expand at a fast rate

drones Unmanned aircraft that are often used for investigation

electrical charge Store of electrical energy in a battery or battery-operated device

electrical current The flow of electricity

electrons Tiny particles that move around the nucleus of an atom

element Substance that cannot be broken down into a simpler substance

emissions The release of substances, especially chemicals, into the atmosphere

energy grid A network of cables or pipes for distributing power

ethical Morally right or acceptable

film A thin layer covering a surface

fuel cells Cells producing an electric current directly from a chemical reaction

galaxies Massive groups of stars and planets

gravity The force that attracts a body toward another body

greenhouse gases Gases that build up in Earth's atmosphere, trapping heat

habitats The natural environments of animals, plants, or other organisms

hybrid Something new created by combining two different things

lasers Machines that use powerful beams of light energy

lawsuits Claims or disputes brought to a court of law to be resolved

light-years One light-year is the distance light travels in one year

meltdown An accident in a nuclear reactor in which the fuel overheats and melts the reactor core

minerals Solid inorganic substances

offshore waters Ocean or seawater some distance from the shore

ore A material from which a metal or valuable mineral can be extracted

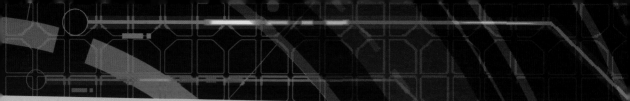

particle physics The branch of science concerned with the nature and properties of matter and energy

policies Courses of action set by a government or business

pollutes Makes dirty, or fills with harmful substances

radiation sickness Illness caused by exposure to radiation

radioactive Materials that give off harmful radiation

sabotage Deliberate damage

silicon A non-metal substance often used in making electronic circuits

terrorists People who use violence to achieve a goal

thermal energy Energy from heat

three-dimensional (3-D) Having three dimensions—height, width, and length

ultrasound Sound that has a frequency too high for the human ear to hear

wavelengths The distances between crests of sounds or light waves

LEARNING MORE

BOOKS

Adams, Kenneth. *Oil Drilling and Fracking* (Earth's Environment in Danger). PowerKids Press, 2018.

Dickmann, Nancy. *Burning Out: Energy from Fossil Fuels* (Next Generation Energy). Crabtree Publishing, 2016.

Herman, Gail. *What Is Climate Change?* (What Was?). Penguin Workshop, 2018.

Kopp, Megan. *Energy from Wind: Wind Farming* (Next Generation Energy). Crabtree Publishing, 2016.

WEBSITES

https://ed.ted.com/lessons/a-guide-to-the-energy-of-the-earth-joshua-m-sneideman
Visit this site to watch a video about the energy of Earth.

www.alternative-energy-news.info/technology/future-energy
Scroll down and click the links on articles about developments in alternative energy.

www.nrcan.gc.ca/energy/efficiency/kidsclub/13760
Visit this site to learn more about energy conservation.

www.ouruniverseforkids.com/cern
Find out more about CERN, an international research center for nuclear research, and watch a movie about the LHC.

INDEX

aquifer 13
artificial intelligence (AI) 19

black holes 37

carbon capture and
    storage (CCS) 20–21
Chernobyl nuclear disaster
    31
climate change 5, 7, 21
concentrated solar power
    (CSP) 16
cosmic rays 39
cyberattacks 9, 33

dark energy 38–39
Deepwater Horizon 9
drones 8

earthquakes 10, 11, 18,
    19, 25, 30
electrons 40
emissions 5, 7, 19, 20, 21,
    44

fossil fuels 4–5, 7, 20, 42,
    43, 44
fracking 10–11, 19
fuel cells 34–35

galaxies 39
geothermal energy 18–19
global warming 5
greenhouse gases 4, 5, 7,
    19, 20, 21, 44

habitats 9
hybrid fission/fusion
    reactor 42–43

Keystone pipelines 12–13

Large Hadron Collider
    (LHC) 36–37, 38, 45

Manhattan Project 26–27
minerals 18, 19

nanotechnology 22–23
nonrenewable energy 4
nuclear disasters 25,
    30–31
nuclear fission 24, 25, 26,
    40, 42, 43
nuclear fusion 24–25,
    40–41, 42–43

offshore drilling 8–9
oil companies 6, 8–9
oil pipelines 5, 6, 8, 12–13

particle accelerators
    36–37, 38, 39
perovskites 32
photovoltaic (PV) cells
    16–17, 32
pipelines 5, 6, 8, 12–13, 20
Pohang earthquake 19

radiation 24–25, 26, 28,
    30, 37
radioactive waste 28–29,
    30, 31, 43
renewable energy 4, 5, 7,
    14, 16, 19, 33, 42, 44

Skunk Works 40–41
smart fabric 22
solar trees 17

thermal energy 16
Three Mile Island 30, 31

U.S. Environmental
    Protection Agency (EPA)
    7

wavelengths 32
wind farms 14, 15

ABOUT THE AUTHOR

Megan Kopp is a freelance writer living in the shadow of the Rocky Mountains. She is a fan of self-powered energy, although she does appreciate the fossil fuels that take her to the hiking, ski, and water trailheads.